Burdened Authority
Leading While In Debt

Authored by
Casey Ray Strong

Acknowledgment

Writing *Burdened Authority* has been a journey of reflection, growth, and discovery. This book would not have been possible without the support, wisdom, and encouragement of many incredible people.

First, I want to thank my family and close friends, whose unwavering belief in my vision kept me grounded through the challenges of writing. Your patience, love, and understanding gave me the strength to keep moving forward.

To the leaders and financial experts who generously shared their insights and experiences, thank you. Your stories and lessons have enriched this book and brought more profound meaning to the connection between debt and leadership.I am also grateful to my mentors and coaches who taught me the importance of integrity, discipline, and resilience; values that are central to the themes explored in this work. I would also like to show my gratitude for the hard work given by my publishing team at Parker Publishers. You all have enhanced this book in many ways.

Lastly, to my readers: thank you for entrusting me with your time and attention. My hope is that *Burdened Authority* will inspire you to lead with clarity, courage, and financial wisdom.

May we all carry our responsibilities with strength, mindful of the burdens we bear and the legacy we leave.

Casey Ray Strong

Dedication

To the steadfast leaders who walk the narrow path of responsibility, bearing burdens unseen yet deeply felt, may this work honor your courage and illuminate your way.

To those who wrestle with the chains of debt, financial and otherwise, may you find here not only understanding, but the strength to break free and lead with renewed clarity and purpose. To the quiet warriors who carry the weight of authority with humility, navigating the storms of challenge and sacrifice, may this book be a beacon of hope and a call to disciplined freedom. May every burden you bear be transformed into a foundation of wisdom, and may your leadership inspire generations to come. Casey Ray Strong

Table of Contents

Introduction

"It's hard to see a clear vision when you cannot breathe."

That's what I muttered to myself one morning, alone, while staring at a stack of unopened bills and a calendar full of meetings I no longer wanted to lead.

I was drowning in a sea of debt.

Not just financial debt—though the credit cards, student loans, and overdraft notices were very real—but also emotional, mental, and spiritual debt. And no one had a clue.

To the outside world, I was strong—a leader, a go-to guy. People came to me for wisdom, support, and ideas. However, on the inside, I was led by fear, making decisions based on what I owed, not what I believed. I smiled through team meetings while silently wondering if this would be the month everything fell apart. Yet I was still making decisions.

Perhaps you are familiar with this feeling.

Maybe you've led the meeting and then cried in your car.

Possibly, you've preached peace while living in a state of panic.

You may have motivated your team while secretly wondering how you would pay the rent.

Perhaps you've said yes to something not because it aligned with your values, but because you were too mentally exhausted to argue.

This book may be for you.

This book is for the leader who is still standing but silently sinking into a sinkhole of debt and worry. It's for those with a heart for people, a vision for growth, and the weight of the world on their shoulders. It's for the one who is tired of pretending that success on the outside means peace on the inside.

Let's tell the truth.

Debt isn't just a financial issue — it is a leadership issue.

It blurs your vision, weakens your voice, steals your sleep and confidence, and eventually erodes your capacity to lead with clarity, compromising your values.

What if there were a different way?

What if the strongest, boldest, most impactful version of your leadership doesn't come from doing more — but from becoming free?

This book isn't just about paying off debt—although we will discuss that, too.

It's about:

- Creating emotional and financial margin
- Reclaiming your voice and, more importantly, your values
- Saying no with strength
- Leading from a clear, quiet, and free center
- Building something that lasts—without losing yourself along the way

You'll read real stories with hard truths. You'll laugh and maybe cry. You'll be challenged to look inward and lead upward. Best of all, you'll be equipped not just to fix numbers on a spreadsheet, but to rise into the kind of leader your life, your family, and your mission deserve.

Here is what I know: When a leader is financially, emotionally, and mentally free, the ripple effect is unstoppable.

You lead your team differently. You parent differently. You make decisions differently.

You become the kind of presence that changes rooms—not through pressure but through peace. Why? You have nothing to hide from. You are not leading as a hypocrite.

We aren't just talking about being debt-free; we are talking about being leadership-ready to the extreme.

So take a breath. Put down the shame. Pick up some tools. And let's walk this road together.

Freedom is calling — not just for your finances but for your leadership.

Let us get started right now.

Chapter 1
The Invisible Burden: How Debt Erodes Confidence and Vision

Leading While Drowning

Marcus was a very respected team leader in a growing nonprofit organization. His board saw his confidence, and he was always composed. To his staff, he was an inspiring and focused leader.

However, Marcus carried $38,000 in credit card debt, a drained savings account, and student loans that had ballooned after continuous deferrals.

Each morning, as he prepared to lead staff meetings or pitch donors, his mind would wander hopelessly.

"How will I cover rent this month?"

"If I mess this up, I lose my job, then what?"

"Can they tell I am panicking on the inside?"

No one knew. Of course, Marcus intended to keep it that way.

The pressure continued to creep silently. He began avoiding crucial decisions. He said yes to projects he should have declined. Marcus overpromised to clients and under delivered to the most important people in his life: his family.

His leadership, once crisp, creative, and anchored, grew reactive and disjointed. Debt didn't just weigh on his finances — it distorted his leadership voice in every aspect of his life. Marcus wasn't weak or dishonest. He was attempting to lead while silently drowning.

The Hidden Cost of Debt in Leadership

Debt isn't just numbers on a balance sheet. It is a narrative, a source of stress, and a distraction.

Debt is a tax on your energy and vision, and it steals your peace right from underneath you.

In leadership, you are continuously expected to make wise, forward-looking decisions. Unfortunately, when debt gets heavy, it drags you into survival mode. It traps you in short-term thinking. It tells your brain: "You are not safe. Fix it Now."

Here's what happens when debt becomes the invisible burden behind a leader's smile:

- Risk Tolerance shrinks – You avoid innovation because you can't afford failure.
- Vision narrows – You make decisions based on next week instead of next year.
- Trust erodes – Not just from others, but deep from within yourself.

- People-pleasing creeps in – You say yes to avoid loss, not to advance purpose.

Since leadership already carries emotional weight, financial fear can tip the scale into burnout, impulsive decisions, or even moral compromise.

Debt doesn't just lower your credit score. It lowers your internal ceiling for confident and effective leadership.

Application for Leaders

Whether your title is parent, manager, entrepreneur, coach, pastor, or something else, you are making high-stakes decisions. Those decisions are most influential when made from clarity, not crisis.

Let's be clear: debt doesn't disqualify you.

But unacknowledged and unmanaged debt weakens you.

When a leader is burdened with silent financial strain, their ability to:

- Say no with confidence.
- Take principled stands.
- Model peace and balance

It becomes severely compromised.

The path forward isn't shame. It is pure strategy.

Tools & Strategies: Reclaiming Margin and Mental Bandwidth

A. Financial Audit with Leadership Lens

Not just what you owe, but how what you owe is affecting what you choose. Ask:

- What decisions have I made due to financial fear?
- Where has debt made me reactive instead of principally reflective?
- How is my leadership voice affected by negative money pressure?

B. Start a "Freedom Fund"

Set aside a small amount of money each week toward an emergency savings or "Freedom fund." I call this the Freedom Fund because it allows you to handle minor emergencies without affecting other bills or your debt reduction budget. Initially, you should fund the Freedom Fund to $1,500.00. Funding the Freedom Fund is the very first thing you need to do within the first 30 days.

C. Externalize the Shame

Speak to a mentor, spouse, advisor, or coach. Naming the pressure breaks its grip. Now is an ideal time to hire a coach and establish a productive working relationship. Isolation feeds fear. However, connection fuels clarity.

Reflection Questions

1. What weight have I been silently carrying that might be affecting my leadership?
2. In what ways has debt (or fear of it) shaped my recent decisions?
3. What would be possible in my leadership if I had no financial anxiety?
4. Who could I invite into my journey that would help toward financial clarity?

"You cannot cast vision when your soul is stuck in survival. Clear the financial fog, and your leadership will rise."

Chapter 2
Self-Mastery Before Strategy
Discipline as the Root of
Leadership

The CEO and the Cracked Foundation

Jennifer had turned her boutique consulting firm into a six-figure business in under three years.

Her reputation was growing, and clients were commenting on her insight. Speaking invitations filled her inbox. But behind the scenes, chaos ruled.

She hadn't paid herself a steady salary in eight months. Her business expenses regularly exceeded her credit card limits. She was overcommitting to client work because she couldn't say no to income. Unfortunately, her staff, though very loyal, constantly waited for delayed reimbursements.

Jennifer's clients admired her brilliance, and her team admired her heart. Unfortunately, her habits were slowly undoing her entire operation.

When her accountant finally intervened, he decided not to use spreadsheets at all. He flat-out told her, "You don't have a money problem. You have a self-discipline problem.". He was absolutely right.

The Unseen Muscle of Great Leaders

Every leadership journey reaches a moment when talent is no longer enough.

At that point, discipline becomes the dividing line between a fleeting flash and a lasting legacy.

It's tempting to define leadership by charisma, influence, or strategy. But a strategy without self-control is like a GPS in a car with no brakes — you'll crash eventually.

Nowhere is discipline more tested — and more visible — than in your finances.

Every budget, every purchase, every yes or no yet reveals whether you're governed by your values or pulled by your impulses.

Great leaders don't just build businesses or movements. They build themselves first.

They cultivate inner architecture: habits, rhythms, and values that create alignment and internal peace.

"Before you can lead the world, you must govern your desires."

Application for Leaders

Think of self-discipline as internal governance. It is the framework of your leadership world:

- Your ability to say no, even when it is unpopular.
- Your ability to delay gratification, especially when it is tempting.
- Your ability to stay and operate within principle while the pressure is deafening.

The more profound truth is this: *"Self-discipline creates freedom of leadership."*

When you are disciplined and lead with it:

- You don't fear financial conversations. You embrace and enjoy them.
- You don't chase clients out of desperation. You provide a space where clients seek you.
- You aren't ruled by shiny objects or tempted by unethical deals.
- You build credibility with yourself. Which builds credibility with everyone.

When it comes to money, every time you align your financial behavior with your long-term values, you become more trustworthy, not just with others but also with yourself. This is what building *"Prosperity Thru Values"* is all about. Never waver or stray from your values, and prosperity will find you.

Strengthening the Discipline Muscle

A. The 10-Second Rule

Before any unplanned purchase or financial commitment, take a step back and pause. Ask:

- Can I afford this with cash?
- Does this align with my values?
- Is this urgent, emergent, or emotional?
- Will I regret this purchase in 72 hours?

That short moment of awareness can be the difference between acting from alignment — or reaction.

If it doesn't align with your values, the answer is no. Always no.

If it aligns with your goals but not your current finances, wait, budget, and purchase later.

The only justifiable exception is true emergency spending.

B. Create "Keystone Habits"

Start with one or two small, repeatable behaviors that build consistency and confidence:

- Review your budget every Monday morning for 10-15 minutes.
- Set a rule: no spending after 8 p.m. without a 24-hour reflection.

- Journal every financial decision you made that day and circle each one you are proud of.
- Write down why you are proud of that financial decision.
- If the purchase exceeds a certain amount, you must hold a budget meeting with your spouse before making the purchase. For my household, that amount is set at $999.00. This process also includes emergency spending.
- Often, at the budget meeting, you will find that it is either not an emergency or that you can conduct some research and find a cheaper alternative.

These habits become your internal governance structure. This structure provides a solid foundation to build upon.

A. Budget to Reflect Your Identity, Not Just Expense

Build a budget that reinforces who you are and what your values represent, not just what you owe:

- If you value generosity, create space for giving.
- If you want freedom, prioritize debt payoff and do it as quickly as possible.
- If you seek Peace, plan for rest.

Make your money a reflection of your life mission. For us, we value many things, but I would like to share with you our budgeting priorities.

- Emergency Fund: When starting an emergency fund, begin by setting aside $1,500. Once you have paid off your debt and are in the phase of making money, you keep 3-6 months' worth of expenses in the fund. Whenever we withdraw from this fund, it is a priority to replenish it. We STOP everything until it reaches the 3-6 months of expenses mark.
- Charity: We save monthly for charity so we can bless people throughout the holidays with unexpected cash donations.
- Investing is the process of allowing our money to earn a return on investment.
- Vacationing and fun money. You have to reward yourself and have some fun.

Reflection Questions

1. Where is my lack of self-discipline costing me Peace or credibility?
2. What financial habit, if changed, would most impact my leadership strength?
3. Do my current habits reflect my long-term vision or my short-term emotions?

4. How do I treat myself when I follow through on what I said I'd do?

"Discipline isn't punishment. It's proof that you believe your future is worth protecting."

Chapter 3
Money as a Mirror, What Spending Reveals About the Leader's Soul

The Leader Who Couldn't Stop Giving

Everyone loved Andrea. They admired her for her generosity. As an executive at a nonprofit and a prominent figure in her community, she never turned down a fundraising dinner, a sponsorship request, or an opportunity to give back by donating to a cause. However, Andrea's financial situation told a different story. Her mortgage was two months behind. She had nothing saved for retirement and hadn't taken a paycheck from her consulting work in over a year. One afternoon, her financial advisor gently asked, "Andrea, what are you trying to prove?"

Tears welled up, and she held her face in her hands. For years, she had equated giving with worth. In her mind, if she stopped giving, people would no longer admire her. Would she even still admire herself?

Andrea didn't have a money management problem; she had a wealth identity problem. Her spending was speaking louder than her voice, and the message it sent was: "I matter because I give."

Spending Is a Spiritual Act

We view money as neutral, objective, or simply a matter of math. In reality, money is rarely just money; it often represents something more. Every spending decision carries emotional, ethical, and identity-driven weight. It reveals:

- What we fear.
- What we crave.
- What we avoid.
- What we truly value.

That's why, for leaders, money is more than just resource management; it's a mirror. It shows who we are and who we are becoming.

The way you handle your finances speaks volumes about:

- Your priorities.
- Your discipline.
- Your Emotional intelligence.
- Your willingness to live in alignment with your values.

"Every dollar spent is a decision made. Over time, those decisions will build your identity."

Application for leaders

Leaders are entrusted with vision. Vision without self-awareness quickly collapses.

If your money habits are shaped by unspoken insecurities, such as a need to appear generous, successful, or in control, your leadership will suffer as a result.

Here is how this shows up:

- Over-giving out of guilt: driven by a need to compensate for past mistakes.
- Overspending for validation: using purchases as proof of worth.
- Avoid budgeting because structure feels like a sense of shame or loss of freedom.
- Inconsistency in generosity: giving to impress, not to impact.

Your financial life should never be a stage. It should be a sanctuary — a place where truth lives, not performance.

Letting the Mirror Teach You

A. Weekly Financial Reflection Journal

Once a week, ask:

- What did I spend money on that felt most aligned with my values?
- What did I buy out of fear, pride, or fatigue?

- What emotions showed up the most this week: scarcity, shame, joy, or Peace?
- This builds pattern recognition and awareness. The two cornerstones of transformation.

B. "Soul Budget" Audit

Look at last month's budget. Categorize each expense under one of the following:

- Value
- Vanity
- Avoidance
- Alignment

No judgment. Just clarity. Then ask: *What Kind of story am I writing with my money?*

C. Establish "Guide Spending Principles"

These are simple, Values-based rules you live by. Examples:

- I never go into debt for a purchase.
- I only give when it's rooted in joy, not guilt
- I save 20% because I lead with future vision, not reaction.

Reflection Questions

1. What recurring financial behavior am I avoiding and why?
2. Where does my spending contradict my stated values as a leader?
3. What do I hope people assume about me based on how I manage my finances?
4. Who could I talk to for honest, shame-free financial feedback?

"Money reveals the truth your mouth may not speak. Let your leadership be one where both align."

Chapter 4
Margin Is the Soil of Wisdom

The Executive With No Space to Think.

A person the people envied was David. His calendar was always booked, his team followed him everywhere with untethered loyalty, and his revenue had doubled in just 18 months. But David was crumbling. He was five years into running his company and six years behind on his rest. David's mornings started with "emergencies," and his evenings ended with a multitude of unfinished tasks. Every decision felt reactive. Every expense felt urgent, and every single day blurred right into the next.

One night, staring at his laptop after midnight, David whispered to himself, "I can't think."

That was the problem. David wasn't losing because of incompetence. He was losing because he allowed others to create a world for him without any margin for error. There was no mental, emotional, or financial space to lead wisely.

Leadership Without Margin Becomes Fragile

Margin is not a luxury. Margin is a leadership infrastructure that must be in place. It is the White space around your decisions. Margin is the pause between stimulus and response. It is the cushion that prevents burnout and invites wisdom.

In a culture obsessed with optimization and hustle, the margin looks weak. In truth, the margin is where:

- Reflection lives.
- Creativity emerges.
- Relationships deepen.
- Clarity has room to speak to you and tells you what you need to hear.

Without margin, leaders lose access to their best thinking, and emotional intelligence vanishes. Worst of all, they lose sight of their values.

"Wisdom does not shout over noise. It whispers into space."

Application for leaders

Margin is more than time management, though. It's a leadership principle that touches your:

- Calendar
- Bank account
- Emotional energy
- Spiritual bandwidth

Leaders without margin tend to:

- Make rushed decisions
- Say yes to the wrong opportunities.

- Overspend to solve problems that clarity could've prevented.
- Burn out and blame others.

Conversely, leaders who protect margin make better hires, create stronger teams, spend with purpose, and navigate stress with resilience.

Margin is not about being idle.

It's about creating room for wisdom to work.

Rebuilding Leadership Margin

A. The "Margin Check" Inventory

Ask yourself at the beginning of every week:

- Do I have 1-2 hours of unscheduled time each day?
- Do I have a 3-month emergency fund?
- Do I feel pressure to say yes because of fear, or am I free to say no with Peace?

B. Budget for Breathing Room

Many budgets are built so tightly that even a minor disruption can cause panic. Build in space and make every dollar you bring in work for you. Allocate EVERY DOLLAR. Start your budget with have-tos:

- Mortgage/Rent
- Utilities

- Insurance
- Groceries
- Car Payment
- Charity
- Investments
- Restaurants
- Vacation
- Christmas
- Date Nights
- His fun money
- Her Fun Money
- Clothing
- Vehicle maintenance
- Miscellaneous

These are line items from mine and Amber's budget. Some may be missing, but we finalize them during our monthly budget meeting—a week before each new month. We ensure every dollar is accounted for and spent intentionally. This is what Dave Ramsey refers to as a zero-dollar budget. We use his app, EveryDollar, and highly recommend it.

C. Schedule Strategic Solitude

Once a week, especially in the beginning, block 60-90 minutes to:

- Reflect on key decisions.
- Review actions that have taken place.

- Ask: What would a wise leader do next?

Don't wait for clarity to interrupt your noise. Create the silence it needs to arrive.

Reflection Questions

1. Where in my life have I traded margin for momentum, and at what cost?
2. What would it look like to lead from rest instead of reaction?
3. How does my limited financial margin restrict my leadership options?
4. What's one margin-creating decision I can make this week?

"Margin isn't wasted space. It's the sacred ground where leadership grows."

Chapter 5
The Budget as Leadership Architecture

The Vision That Couldn't Breathe

Tasha was a visionary. As the founder of a small social enterprise, she had bold ideas, contagious passion, and a clear mission: transforming her city through ethical employment. But there was a problem. Every month ended in financial chaos. Payroll was a stress test, to put it mildly. Vendor bills piled up, she avoided reviewing her expenses and explained it to herself by saying, 'We are doing God's work." Though that may be true, the money doesn't ever work itself out, no matter whose work you're doing. Of course, it never did.

After laying off two team members unexpectedly, a coach sat her down and said, "Tasha, your budget isn't just about survival. It is a blueprint of your leadership."

Until that moment, she had viewed budgeting as a reactive process, something to do after the fact. Of course, she needed an intentional design; her mission wasn't failing, but her architecture was.

Budgets Are Not Just Plans; They Are Principles in Action

Too often, budgets feel like diets: restrictive, joyless, and destined to be broken. But a good budget is permission to spend and a leadership tool.

It's not just about where your money goes—it's about what your money is building.

Budgets do three things:

1. Clarify Priorities: They reveal what you truly value, not what you claim to value.
2. Reveal Leaks: They show where unconscious habits or emotional decisions are undermining your goals.
3. Enable Trust: They empower others to follow your leadership because they see structure and not chaos.

You cannot lead with strength if your money is managed by stress.

"A clear budget is the scaffolding of a sustainable vision."

Application for Leaders

As a leader, your financial decisions are not personal; they are cultural. People watch how you spend:

- Do you invest in what matters?
- Do you model delayed gratification?
- Do you protect resources for long-term goals?

Whether you lead a household, a team, a non-profit, or a business, your budget teaches others how to think. It says:

- Here's what we build.
- Here's how we grow,
- Here's what we don't chase, even when it is tempting.

When your money aligns with your mission, your leadership becomes unshakeable.

Designing a Budget That Leads

A. Build with Vision, Not Just Categories

Before inputting numbers, ask yourself:

- What are my top 3 leadership priorities this year?
- How can my budget reflect and support those priorities?

Let your vision lead your math. Don't go into debt to lead. That constitutes failure. When you build the budget and allow your vision to guide your math, you will be able to place proper line items in your budget that demonstrate your leadership intent.

B.   Allocate in Seasons, Not Just Months

Leadership flows in rhythm. Once you have your monthly budget down, which is fluid, create a quarterly budget map:

- What are your investment needs this season?
- What needs to rest?
- Where do we need to maintain a margin or savings to prepare for growth?

C.   Share selectively, Lead Publicly.

If you lead a team or even your family:

- Share parts of the budget to foster ownership.
- Model financial decisions with transparency.
- Celebrate alignment more than accumulation.

Your budget doesn't just manage money; it also manages your finances. It will train the culture you want as your values will be followed.

Reflection Questions

1. What is my current budget unintentionally prioritizing?

2. Where is my money supporting comfort over calling?
3. What is one category I need to redefine and realign?
4. If someone were to study my budget, what would they say I value most?
5. Do I have a coach? Why not?

"A mission without a budget is a dream. A budget without a mission is a trap. When they align, they become a movement."

Chapter 6
The Emotional Economics of Leadership

The CFO Who Couldn't Sleep

Richard was a high-performing CFO. By day, he analyzed balance sheets, made million-dollar forecasts, and consulted on capital strategy. At night, however, he lay awake, staring at the ceiling, haunted by a different set of numbers, his own.

Despite his expertise, Richard carried $120,000 in consumer debt. He earned enough to pay it down, but he never did. His financial life was an emotional minefield of guilt, pride, fear of judgment, and shame for not "Knowing better." Unfortunately, this is very common.

He made rational decisions for his company. When it came to his own life, it was ruled purely by emotions. Richard didn't need another spreadsheet. He needed to process the emotional economics that were running his private show and silently undermining his leadership. He needed a coach.

Money Decisions Are Rarely Logical; They Are Emotional First

Behavioral economists have proven that most financial decisions begin in the limbic system, the emotional center of the brain. Logic often shows up too late after fear, guilt, or desire has already hijacked the decision. Stepping back and taking a breath helps the decision-making process. This is also the reason for high-pressure buy-now sales pitches. They work.

For leaders, this creates a dangerous gap. You can be:

- Wise in strategy but weak in personal stewardship.
- Principled in public yet reactive in private.
- Visionary in goals but sabotaged by unexamined patterns.

You don't outgrow emotional money decisions by becoming richer. You outgrow them by being self-aware. By being self-aware, you can take the additional time to think. Is this an emotional or logical response? Is this a need or a want? By asking those questions, you are taking the time and due diligence needed to help set aside that emotional urge to spend, spend, spend.

"Until you heal the emotion driving your spending, your money will always manage you."

Application for Leaders

You are not just making financial decisions; You are modeling emotional regulations.

If your team, family, or mentees see impulsive spending, chronic guilt, or financial avoidance, they will follow suit. Even if they respect your vision. Every emotional pattern you don't address becomes a leadership liability:

- Scarcity mindsets create hoarding cultures.
- Shame creates secrecy and silos.
- Overgiving from guilt leads to burnout.
- Avoidance turns minor issues into crises.

Emotionally aware leaders lead calmly in crisis, spend with clarity and purpose, and model both empathy and discipline.

Rewiring Emotional Patterns Around Money

A. Emotion Before Action

Before a financial decision, pause. Ask:

- Is this an emotional purchase?
- What emotion am I feeling and why?
- Am I purchasing to avoid something deeper?
- Would this decision look different if I felt safe and confident?

- Does this fit within the budget, or do I need to go outside it?
- Do I need this now, or can I budget for it?

Asking these questions, as well as adding at least a 30-second pause in between answers, can save you years of regret. This process will also bring out the leader in you, influencing whether you make the purchase or not. It will tuck the emotional little kid away where they belong.

B. Name Your Financial Triggers

Common emotional triggers:

- Insecurity = Overcompensating with status purchases
- Guilt = Overgiving to feel worthy of others.
- Fear = Hoarding instead of investing
- Shame = Avoiding budgeting or feedback

Whatever the trigger, naming it will neutralize its power.

C. Rewrite the Narrative

Use this 3-step method:

1. Name the old story: "I'm not smart with money."
2. Replace with a truth: "I'm learning to lead myself with integrity."

3. Act from the new story: "One aligned decision reinforces the truth."

Transformation happens through repetition, not resolution. Get yourself a coach.

Reflection Questions

1. What emotion most often drives my financial behavior?
2. When did I first learn that money was tied to self-worth, safety, or shame?
3. What's one emotional pattern I'm ready to replace with a principle/Value?
4. Who can I process these truths with, free from judgment?
5. Why do I not have a coach?

"Leadership isn't about hiding your emotions. It's about understanding them and refusing to let them drive your financial decisions."

Chapter 7
The Cost of Compromise
Integrity Over Image
in Leadership

The Nonprofit Leader Who Lost Her Way

Rachel founded a nonprofit with a powerful mission: to serve inner-city youth through mentorship and education. The community believed in her. Donors believed in her. For a while, her impact matched the vision.

Somewhere along the way, she started cutting corners. She stretched the grant report to make the numbers appear more favorable. She used organizational credit for personal expenses, telling herself, "I'll pay it back soon." She hired a friend over a qualified candidate to avoid conflict. Each decision felt small. They felt justified and necessary under the circumstances.

Until one donor pulled out. Then another. When the truth came to light, so did the damage, not just to her organization but also to her leadership reputation.

Rachel never set out to be unethical.

She set out to keep the dream alive. However, she sacrificed her integrity to do it. She turned away from her values.

Compromise Always Costs More Than It Promises.

Compromise doesn't start with big betrayals. It seems to always start with tiny rationalizations:

- I deserve this after what I've endured
- No one will notice
- Just this once, to make the numbers work
- I will pay it back before anyone ever notices

However, small cracks in integrity can lead to structural collapse over time.

For leaders, the greatest threat is not failure; failure is a given in leadership. It's erosion.

Erosion happens when the image becomes more important than alignment.

"When leaders trade principle for convenience, they mortgage their legacy for temporary peace."

Application for Leaders

As a leader, you are not just managing decisions; you are stewarding trust.

Compromise, especially in financial matters, signals to others:

- That outcomes matter more than values.
- That results in excused shortcuts.
- That "whatever it takes" is an acceptable creed.

This type of culture seeps into teams, marriages, and organizations. It then spreads like cancer, and soon, no one knows where the lines are. Everyone is guessing, values are lost, and trust decays until it is completely gone.

However, when you model financial integrity, even when it is slow, complex, and perhaps painful, you give people something truly priceless: security in your leadership.

Guarding Against Financial Compromise

A. **Create Personal "Non-Negotiables"**

Before a crisis hits, define what is off limits:

- No use of business funds for personal reasons.
- No fudging numbers, EVER.
- No spending that violates shared values, even if legal.

Clear lines always reduce any blurry moments.

B. **Conduct Quarterly Integrity Audits**

Once per quarter, ask:

- Have I rationalized anything recently?
- Is my private financial behavior aligned with my public role?
- Am I hiding anything from people I trust?

What you confess in Peace won't destroy you in crisis.

C. Surround Yourself with Truth-Tellers

Invite at least one mentor, advisor, friend, or, preferably, a coach to ask you regularly.

- Are you still walking in alignment?
- Their courage protects your credibility.

Reflection questions

1. Where have I been tempted to compromise "just this once"?
2. What system or standard do I need to strengthen to avoid blurry ethics?
3. Who in my life could lovingly call me back to the truth if I wavered?
4. What part of my legacy would be lost if I exchanged principle for pressure?
5. Do I have a coach?

"At the moment, compromise feels like a relief. In the long run, it reveals what you were willing to lose to avoid discomfort."

Chapter 8
Leadership Habits Forged in Financial Freedom

The Quiet Rise of a Consistent Man

Every morning at 5:30 a.m., Thomas brewed his coffee, reviewed his budget, prayed over his business, and reviewed the day's client list. For 12 years, this quiet, unassuming financial coach built a company that served thousands, stayed debt-free, and empowered his community.

There are no viral moments. No overnight success. Just relentless discipline.

When asked how he created such a legacy, Thomas replied, "I built a few small habits, then kept showing up." "That's it."

Freedom Isn't a Feeling, It's a Pattern

Many believe that financial freedom is about achieving a specific goal, such as achieving zero debt, accumulating six-figure savings, or retiring early. Absolute freedom isn't just a status; it's a state of being. It's a system of behavior.

It is created and sustained by the habits you live out every day. These aren't just money habits. They are leadership rhythms that reflect the following:

- Your discipline
- Your clarity
- Your integrity
- Your commitment to future vision over present emotion.

"What you do consistently reveals who you are becoming permanently."

Habits matter because character is not built in crises. It's revealed by what you've rehearsed in ordinary moments.

Application for Leaders

Your team, family, and peers may not share your goals. They follow your rhythms.

If you spend impulsively, you learn that leadership is reactive. If you reflect, budget, and build margin, you learn leadership is intentional.

Freedom-minded leaders:

- Review their finances without shame.
- Make decisions from systems, not moods.
- Honor their commitments, even when they are made privately.

- Build patterns of rest, review, generosity, and foresight.

Habits create the infrastructure of integrity. Without them, even the best vision crumbles under pressure.

Habits That Build Financially Grounded Leadership

A. Daily Habits

- **5-Minute Money Check-In:** Log one financial win or insight daily.
- **Budget Reminder:** Read your "WHY" and the purpose behind your spending plan.
- **Discipline Anchor:** One intentional act of restraint or generosity each day.

B. Weekly Habits

- **Money Meeting:** With spouse or coach, review, adjust, and affirm alignment
- **Financial Faithfulness Review:** Ask, "Did I live what I believe financially this week?"
- **Pre-Decide the Weekend:** Plan for joy, not regret. Budget fun, rest, and recovery.

C. Monthly Habits

- **Freedom Forecast:** Project 90 days out; plan for giving, saving, and surprises.
- **Legacy Ledger:** Review whether your spending is building what you want to leave.

- **Celebrate Growth:** Even $50 of progress deserves acknowledgment.

These habits may seem small, but they foster resilient, value-driven leadership. This is what builds prosperity thru values.

Reflection Questions

1. Which of my daily habits reinforces financial clarity, and which sabotages it?
2. What story is my current routine telling my family, team, or clients?
3. Where am I waiting for motivation instead of relying on discipline?
4. What's one habit I can start this week to become more financially free?
5. Do I have a coach?

"Discipline isn't a punishment. It's the daily vote for the leader you're becoming."

Chapter 9
Generational Wealth, Not Just for the Wealthy

The Legacy of a Janitor

When James passed away at age 88, he left behind no heirs: just a modest house, a stack of well-worn ledgers, and stories of kindness.

James had worked as a janitor at the same elementary school for 43 years. He never made more than $30,000 in a single year. When his will was opened, the town was stunned; he had left behind nearly $2 million that he had saved, invested, and earmarked for scholarships and youth centers.

His habits were quiet. His life was simple. His impact? Generational.

James proved that wealth isn't about income; it is about intentionality.

Legacy Begins Long Before You Die

We often confuse generational wealth with trust funds, stock portfolios, and real estate. Those are just tools. True legacy is built on principles, practices, and priorities passed from one generation to the next. "Prosperity Thru Values"

It includes:

- Financial literacy
- Character-driven decision-making
- Generosity that flows through generations
- Stories that shape identity and vision

You don't need a high net worth to pass wealth on. You need a high-trust blueprint that others can follow.

"Generational wealth is not what you leave for people. It's what you leave in them."

Application for Leaders

Whether you are a parent, mentor, business owner, coach, or teacher, you are shaping someone's future model for:

- How to handle money
- How to define success
- How to recover from mistakes
- How to think about giving, building, and stewarding

If you don't lead these lessons with intention and purpose, society will fill the gap, often with consumerism, anxiety, and a sense of entitlement. This is your opportunity to lead by example and teach people around you how to be the best version of themselves.

You don't need millions to leave a legacy.

You need clarity, courage, purpose, and discipline.

Building Legacy Now

A. Define Your Wealth Vision

Ask yourself:

- What financial values do I want my children, mentees, or employees to embody?
- What money principles or values do I want to outlast me?
- What is enough for me, and what kind of impact do I want to have on others?
- What does Prosperity Thru Values look like for me?

Write it down. Share it with others. Let your people see your blueprint.

B. Teach While You Build

Legacy isn't inherited. It's taught. By living Prosperity Thru Values and teaching those around you, a Legacy will be passed on.

- Involve your kids in budget meetings. They will take unbelievable actions.
- Let your mentees see your generosity in action.
- Share why you saved, not just what you saved.
- Share the value of having no debt and having no payments.

It is not enough to leave money. You must leave meaning.

C. Create a Transfer Plan

This could be very simple:

- A notebook with financial lessons and family values. We know this isn't taught by anyone else.
- A video series for your future grandchildren
- A will that reflects not just wealth but also wisdom. Wisdom is a fantastic gift for anyone to give and even more amazing to receive.

Don't just pass down assets. Pass down the anchoring truth that will continue to teach and lead for generations to come.

Reflection Questions

1. What am I doing today that is shaping someone's financial mindset?
2. What would I want my great-grandchildren to believe about money and leadership?
3. What stories, values, or systems can I begin documenting now?
4. Am I more focused on leaving stuff or building Prosperity Thru Values?

"Wealth doesn't start with a paycheck. It starts with a principle, passed faithfully from one generation to the next."

Chapter 10
The Family Economy
Leading at Home
As You Lead at Work

CEO at Work, Chaos at Home

Maria ran a $4 million company. Her team operated like a Swiss watch: budgets, KPIs, culture meetings, vision casting, and the whole nine yards. She trained leaders globally on alignment and clarity.

At Home?

Late bills. Unspoken money stress. Weekly arguments with her husband. Her kids thought "budget" meant punishment. Her finances were strong, but her family was fractured. This is not an unusual phenomenon, either, when it comes to CEOs and high-level executive leaders.

It hit her one night when her 11-year-old asked, " Are we poor or rich?"

Maria froze. She had mastered strategic leadership in the boardroom. However, she ignored it in the living room.

A Family Without Financial Leadership Is a Company Without a CEO

Most families function as individuals and not as a team. Spending happens reactively. Roles are undefined, and conversations are avoided. The result?

- Misunderstandings
- Mistrust
- Missed opportunities to build a legacy.

The same principles that lead great teams also build great households:

- Clear values
- Shared goals
- Open communication
- Trust through transparency

"You can outsource your finances, but you cannot outsource the culture you create around money at home."

Your home is the first economy you lead. Do it on purpose with intention. Remember, "Prosperity Thru Values."

Application for Leaders

Whether you're leading a partner, children, roommates, or even a household of one, financial harmony requires intentional leadership.

Here is what often goes wrong:

- One person leads, and the other resents
- No one leads, and conflict festers until it blows up.
- Children grow up confused, inheriting silence and shame instead of clarity and values.
- Marriages often end due to a lack of communication, which can lead to financial conflicts.

But it doesn't have to be that way at all.

When you build your family economy, you build:

- Teamwork.
- Emotional security.
- Stewardship values that outlive you.
- A line of communication that is rarely taught.

It's not about being perfect with money. It is about being present and aligned.

Designing a Strong Family Economy

A. Define Financial Roles Together

It is imperative to sit down and assign the following roles:

- When is the monthly budget meeting?
- Who manages the day-to-day budget?

- What amount requires a budget meeting before making a purchase?
- How do we involve the children appropriately?
- What constitutes an emergency?

Clarity prevents resentment. You can add anything you need to this list.

B. Start Monthly "Budget or Money& Vision Dates"

Make it positive, not punitive. This should be a fun thing to do. Agenda:

- What worked last month?
- What needs adjustment?
- Do we need to add or subtract any categories?
- What are we celebrating or preparing for?
- What is our giving amount?

C. Teach Kids in Layers

- Ages 3-6: Money comes from work. Saving is wise.
- Ages 7-12: Budgeting, giving, and earning lessons.
- Teens: Bank accounts, investments, delayed gratification, and generosity principles.

Your children's future confidence is built on today's consistent modeling.

Reflection Questions

1. Is my home led with as much intentionality as my work or team?
2. What financial assumptions or stressors are going unspoken in my household?
3. What do I want my children or partner to remember about how we managed our finances?
4. What is one step I can take this week to create unity around our finances?

"Lead your home like you lead your mission, with clarity, courage, and a shared vision."

Chapter 11
Sacred Conversations
Talking About Money With Grace and Courage

The Silence That Cost Everything

DeShawn and Lydia were in love, shared a similar faith, and were deeply committed to their future. To their detriment, they never really talked about money. They assumed it would all work out, after all. They were both responsible adults. Until it didn't. Three years into their marriage, DeShawn discovered Lydia had $60,000 in credit card debt. Lydia found that DeShawn had been secretly gambling, and neither of them had shared their financial truths. They both feared judgment, conflict, and rejection. Now, their trust was shattered.

They didn't fall apart due to financial constraints. They fell apart because of secrecy. They never communicated what they needed to.

Money Conversations Are Never Just About Math

Talking about money is talking about:

- Trust
- Power

- Fear
- Identity
- Forgiveness

Which means it requires more than just spreadsheets. It requires emotional fluency, empathy, courage, and sincere communication. Most people carry unresolved money stories from childhood:

- "We never talked about money."
- "Money was always tight, so it was always stay quiet and not ask."
- "If you make more, you're better."

When these stories collide in relationships, they create confusion, resentment, and emotional gridlock. The only way to prevent this from happening is to rewrite the script. Be completely honest and put EVERYTHING on the table. Work through the negatives and come up with a plan TOGETHER.

"Financial conversations are not accounting tasks. They are acts of leadership and love."

Application for Leaders

Whether you're in a marriage, business partnership, family system, or team, how you discuss money reveals the health of the culture you're creating and maintaining.

- Avoidance breeds anxiety

- Blame breed defensiveness
- Clarity breeds confidence
- Consistency builds trust

Sacred conversations are those that hold tension gently. They allow truth but consistently deliver it with grace. They seek understanding before the agreement. A financially free leader doesn't just manage money well; they communicate about it honestly and redemptively. An economically free leader will always get to the why of financial mistakes.

Leading Healthy Financial Dialogue

A. **Learn Each Other's "Money Blueprint."**

Start with curiosity, not criticism. Ask the following:

- What's your first memory of money?
- What did your family teach (or not teach) about money?
- What's your biggest fear when it comes to finances?

B. **Use "We Language."**

Avoid "you always" and "you never." Instead, ask:

- How can we make these decisions together?

- What does OUR vision look like this season?
- Let's face this debt as a team.
- What does Prosperity Thru Values look like to us?

Approach the mistakes with unity instead of blame.

C. Schedule the Talk: Don't Make It a Surprise.

Pick a set time each month for a Money Check-in or Budget Committee meeting:

- Set the atmosphere: calm, open, device-free.
- Stick to an agenda: gratitude, updates, goals, challenges.
- End with something kind: appreciation, affirmation, and prayer

Money conversations and budget meetings should build connection, not anxiety.

Reflection Questions

1. What money story or fear am I still carrying, and how does it manifest in my conversations?
2. When was the last time I had a grace-filled, honest talk about finances?
3. Who do I avoid talking to about money, and why?

4. What would change if I saw financial dialogue as sacred instead of scary?

Chapter 12
The Leadership Legacy Map
Systems, Succession,
and Significance

The Empire That Died With the Founder

Elijah built an empire. From humble beginnings, he launched a consulting firm that employed dozens, helped thousands, and influenced national leaders. His face was on magazine covers. His voice was respected in every room he entered.

When Elijah passed unexpectedly at 62, something devastating happened:

The business collapsed within a year. He never put an emergency plan in place. He had no systems, no succession plan, and no transferable wisdom. What took decades to build unraveled in just a couple of months because Elijah never mapped his legacy beyond his presence.

If It Can't Outlive You, It's Not Legacy, It's Nothing More Than a Project

Authentic leadership isn't proven by how much you control; it's demonstrated by how much you empower others. It's proven by how well the thing you built continues without you.

Many leaders assume legacy is about:

- End-of-life planning
- Wills and inheritance
- A significant donation or a named scholarship

However, legacy isn't an event. It's a design, a system of people, values, and strategies that carry your influence forward. You can either lead your legacy intentionally or leave others guessing.

"Legacy isn't what you leave behind. It's what you leave built, alive, and multiplying in others."

Application for Leaders

Whether you lead a company, family, church, or community initiative, your legacy depends on three key elements:

1. **Systems** – Do you have repeatable, teachable methods that others can follow?
2. **Succession** – Are you raising and equipping others to lead after you?
3. **Significance** – Are you clear on the why that makes all of this matter?

If any of these are missing, you risk burnout, or worse, building a platform that dies with your name and never lives on after you.

Your leadership should be replicable, not just re-markable. Lead and mentor those who will succeed you in your leadership position.

Mapping Your Leadership Legacy

A. Build Transferable Systems

Ask yourself:

- If I were gone for 90 days, what would fall apart?
- What knowledge, workflow, or process needs to be documented, delegated, or automated?
- Systemize not to replace people but to empower them to replace you in the future.

B. Identify and Equip Successors

Who can carry the mission forward? Start now:

- Hold mentorship meetings
- Delegate decisions
- Shadow your thinking, not just your tasks

Legacy is a relay race, not a solo sprint.

C. Define Your Significance Statement

Write a legacy purpose in 1-2 sentences:

- I want to be remembered for…
- I hope my work teaches others that…
- The impact I care most about is…

Use this as your leadership North Star, and filter future goals through this statement.

Reflection Questions

1. What have I built that could be sustained or replicated without me?
2. Who is learning from me, not just what I do, but how I think and why?
3. What systems or values do I want to pass down in written, teachable form?
4. Is my current pace building a legacy or just maintaining a name?

"Your leadership won't be measured by applause. It will be measured by how well it echoes in others after you're gone."

Chapter 13
Stewardship as Strategy
Leading with What You've Been Given

The Coach Who Did More With Less

Danielle didn't have much. Her youth program operated out of a rented church basement. Her budget was a shoestring. Her staff? Mostly volunteers. Despite all of that, in five years, she graduated over 300 teens with scholarships, job skills, and renewed confidence.

When asked how she managed to do so much with so little, Danielle replied, "I don't lead from what I lack; I lead from what I have been given." She had learned the secret: Stewardship is not about the size of the resources but the strength of the response.

Stewardship Isn't Maintenance, It's Multiplication

Most people treat stewardship as passive:

- "Protect what you have."
- "Don't mess it up."
- "Play it safe."

Amazingly, real stewardship is active, bold, and visionary.

It asks:

- How can I multiply what's been placed in my hands?
- How do I bring value to what I didn't choose but was chosen to manage?
- How do I bring them together without ruining them?

You may not control the size of your platform, budget, team, or time. However, you can control your response to each one of them.

"Leadership is not about what you hold. It's about how you hold it."

Application for Leaders

Too often, we delay impact because we're waiting on:

- More money
- More time
- Better people
- Ideal conditions

But stewardship asks a better question:

What can I do excellently with what I already have?

This mindset does three things:

1. **Reclaims power** – You stop blaming external lack and start building internal momentum.
2. **Generates trust** – People follow leaders who maximize what they're given.
3. **Invites expansion** – Faithful stewardship attracts more opportunity.

You don't need a miracle to move forward. You need a mindset shift from ownership to **entrustment**.

Stewardship That Scales

A. Do a Resource Reframe Audit

Take inventory of what you do have:

- Time (even 30 minutes a day)
- Talents (even if underutilized)
- Relationships (mentors, allies, team)
- Tools (software, books, knowledge, experience)

Now ask: "What is the highest and best use of each of these this season?"

B. Lead with Gratitude, Not Guilt

Many leaders burn out because they feel like stewards must suffer. But good stewardship includes:

- Rest
- Joy
- Celebration
- Honoring progress, not just results.

Gratitude fuels better decisions than pressure ever will.

C. Multiply Through Mentorship

Your influence expands when you teach others to steward what you've learned.

- Coaching a new leader
- Document a system
- Pass down insight before the position.
- Teach people to be your replacement and those above you.

This is how stewardship becomes strategy.

Reflection Questions

1. Where have I been focused on what I lack instead of what I have?
2. What resources have I been underutilizing out of fear or uncertainty?
3. Who can I serve or mentor to multiply my current impact?
4. How would my leadership shift if I saw everything I have as a sacred trust?

"What you do with what you've been given reveals what you believe about the giver."

Chapter 14
The Daily Rhythm of Financially
Free Leaders

The Rhythm That Rebuilt a Life

After surviving a financial collapse and personal burnout, Malik didn't try to "crush" his following goals. He didn't jump to hustle mode or set 20 new intentions.

He started small. Each morning: Coffee, a quiet moment, five minutes reviewing his budget. Each evening: a short gratitude list, a journal entry about the day's money choices, and a prayer of realignment.

One day turned into ten. Ten into sixty. Within a year, Malik paid off $24,000 in debt, rebuilt his confidence, and found Peace for the first time in decades. When asked how he did it, he said, "I didn't just change my finances. I also changed my rhythm."

Your Rhythm is Your Leadership Operating System

Leaders often become obsessed with goals, significant milestones, and breakthrough moments. This obsession can be unhealthy if action is not taken in the right areas. The secret to transformation is not in the goal. It is in the daily rhythm.

Rhythm creates:

- Consistency without burnout
- Confidence without perfection
- Peace without stagnation

Financially free leaders aren't free because of one big win. They are free because they've rehearsed small wins every day in thought, choice, and character. They then put these rehearsals into daily action.

"The freedom you want isn't found in a future number. It's formed in today's pattern."

Application for Leaders

You're not just managing money. You're building daily alignment with your vision.

Most leaders make the mistake of only checking in financially when things are urgent, bills are due, unexpected expenses arise, or big purchases are made. A proactive rhythm changes the game completely.

A healthy rhythm in your financial leadership leads to the following:

- Lower stress
- Higher awareness
- Stronger self-trust
- Compound growth in your results and habits.

When your rhythm is correct, your decisions become clearer, faster, and freer, aligning with your values. This is how we build prosperity thru values.

Building a Leadership Rhythm That Sustains

A. Morning Alignment Ritual (10 Minutes)

- Read your budget or goal statement aloud.
- Visualize one financial decision you'll make aligned with your values.
- Speak a declaration: "I have enough; I lead with wisdom. I choose what builds a legacy."

B. Midday Pulse Check (2 Minutes)

- Ask: "Have I made any reactive financial choices today?"
- If yes, adjust. If not, affirm and stay on the course.

C. Evening Reflection (10 Minutes)

- Journal: One win, one challenge, one insight
- Review account activity, not for shame, but for stewardship
- Practice gratitude for any act of restraint, clarity, or generosity

D. Weekly Rhythm Reset (30-60 Minutes)

- Celebrate progress

- Update budget/goals
- Reconnect with your "why."
- Plan spending and giving for alignment.

Rhythm doesn't control you; it supports you.

Reflection Questions

1. What's the first thing I do in the morning, and how does it shape my mindset for financial leadership?
2. Where do I feel most out of sync, and what rhythm would help restore my alignment?
3. How can I create a system that celebrates small wins without striving for perfection?
4. Who in my life models rhythm overreaction, and what can I learn from them?

"Freedom is not a finish line. It's a rhythm you repeat until Peace becomes your default."

Chapter 15
Leadership Without the Leash: Finishing Debt-Free, Living Fully Free

The Finish Line That Felt Like a Beginning

After 17 years of slow and steady effort, Bianca clicked the "submit" button on her final debt payment. No confetti, no big announcement. Just a quiet breath she hadn't realized she'd been holding for nearly two decades. That night, she and her husband danced in the kitchen, feeling the weight of debt had been lifted from their shoulders. She said, "I thought being debt-free would mean I'm done. But it doesn't feel like an ending. It feels like I can finally lead without fear. I'm truly free to build what matters."

Bianca didn't just escape debt; she reclaimed her leadership, her clarity, her capacity, and her call.

Debt Isn't Just Financial. It's Emotional and Spiritual

Debt acts like a leash. Even when you have vision, strength, or a calling, it tugs you back:

- It clouds your decisions.
- It limits your generosity.
- It forces short-term choices.

- It steals your rest.

When you remove the leash, what's left? A leader who can think long, give deeply, and build boldly without fear of failure.

"Being debt-free doesn't just change your wallet. It changes your walk."

You lead differently when you owe no one anything.

- You speak more clearly.
- You invest smarter.
- You live more lightly.

Application for Leaders

Living debt-free gives leaders:

- Margin for better decisions
- Confidence to wait, not react
- Room to be generous without guilt
- Energy to pursue purpose instead of a paycheck

Freedom, though, is not just financial; it's foundational.

It says:

- "I lead my life, not the lender."
- "I choose vision, not pressure."
- "I no longer build from fear."

Debt-free leadership isn't about having millions of dollars. It's about removing what restricts your mission.

Living Fully Free After Debt

A. Redefine Wealth Beyond Numbers

Ask yourself:

- What am I now free to say yes to?
- Who can I serve now that I'm not burdened?
- What can I finally build without compromise?

Freedom is not the finish line; it is your foundation.

B. Set New Rhythms, Not New Limits

Many people replace old debt with new spending. Don't do it. Instead:

- Maintain a margin-based budget.
- Practice intentional rest and generosity.
- Continue to make decisions based on your leadership values.

C. Teach What You've Lived

The best way to reinforce freedom is to share it:

- Mentor someone

- Write down your journey.
- Give generously and strategically.

Turn your journey into a pathway for others.

Reflection Questions

1. What would it look like to lead every part of my life like I'm already free?
2. Where do I still feel tied down, and what belief or behavior needs to shift to move forward?
3. How can I utilize my freedom to amplify my impact on others?
4. What does "finishing well" mean to me, and am I on that path?

"Freedom isn't just the absence of debt. It's the presence of purpose, Peace, and power in how you lead."

Conclusion
Freedom Is the Foundation,
Not the Finish Line

You didn't read this book because you simply wanted to pay off debt. You read it because deep down, you know this truth:

A leader who is free leads differently.

Not just financially free but emotionally free. Spiritually clear. Aligned with purpose. Grounded in values. Courageous under pressure. Intentional in rhythm. Unshakable when storms come. Finally, someone who has reached "Prosperity Thru Values."

The journey to debt freedom is not just about money. It's about who you become on your journey:

- Someone who tells the truth, not just pays the bills.
- Someone who builds a legacy instead of chasing success.
- Someone who leads with integrity, not performance alone
- Someone who teaches by doing, not just talking.

Financial freedom is not the goal.

From here, you are called to:

- Build homes of Peace.
- Lead teams with clarity.
- Shape cultures of stewardship.
- Fund missions that matter.
- Walk boldly, speak loudly, and give without fear.

You are no longer tethered to anxiety, images, or the opinions of others. You are free to lead from vision, not from survival.

In doing so, you give others permission to do the same and seek the wonders of living with **"Prosperity Thru Values."**

www.ingramcontent.com/pod-product-compliance
Lightning Source LLC
Chambersburg PA
CBHW051233120626
46547CB00013B/1623